How many kids do I have?
Let's see, that depends on how you count them.
Two first trimesters and three clinically removed.
But hey what's it to you?
This is my body,
my mind,
my soul,
….if I don't repent.
Tell your god I never asked for his gifts.
I never asked for Eve to eat fruit, because she ate
it, we bear it?
Cursed as a woman, we are cursed by god.
Women submit to your husbands while they to no
one.
Oh how life would be easier if I had to stand while
I pissed.
I am so sick of this bias world.
The men own it.
We're just like the animals under his dominion.
We're under his control, it seems we're only useful
when we're under his pole.

The Curse

I miss you so much,
it's like my heart is tearing.

I have faith in our love
and faith in how you looked at me.
I have faith in that genuine smile
I use to put on your face.

I believe,
you will remember those days.
I believe,
you never forgot.
You just moved them,
you suppressed them.
Whatever the reason,
 it doesn't change the fact
that I never stopped loving you.

I asked God if it was vain
 then remove it from me.
 I asked God if it was a soul tie
 then break it.
You're still here in my heart,
I know it all makes sense.
We made sense,
we worked.

Everyone knew you'd marry me.
I want to believe.

I want to see
our love achieve,
but how long does it take?
How long must I wait
for you?

These aches
Don't go away.
I love you, for you.
I refuse,
to love another
when my other
half is you.

My soul mated with yours,
there's no divorce.
You're near me at any length.
Our hearts beat at the same rhythm
and bleed with distance.
Don't leave me even for a second.

I resent you so much,
it's like my heart is repairing.

Wife

So sick I just wish you'd go ahead and die.
I'm just tired of being tied.
I no longer want to be your wife.
I regret the day I said I do.
I don't. I don't, I don't, love you.

I did your part and mine.
And you never even took the time,
to say thank you. You're appreciated.
Just leave me unwanted and decapitated.

If dinner isn't done, if a bill isn't paid
off with her head, I'll just screw the maid.
Cheating, lying, disrespectful, bastard.
Oh, at your funeral there will not be a pastor.

I will not bring up anyone who would lie for you.
To say that you were noble, a good man, and true.
Hell no, I am going to tell the truth.
He ate away at people's bodies and souls.
So God gave him a plague that would do both.

Gogh

Maybe I'm delusional,
I've lost sight of what love is.
Is it even still possible for you to love me?

I was always in the picture,
so how come I was the one pushed from the
frame?
Me.

I'm only guilty of one and that's you.
I think of you daily, this is unhealthy.
But they're good thoughts, it feels wrong.

 I try to convince myself that you are bad,
 so maybe I'll see all the reasons we aren't meant,
I gotta move on.

Silly me, I hear your heart not your talk.
I see your intentions not your actions.
Hear I go again, delusional.

Delusionally in love - that's me.

Five Questions

What is a soul mate?
Does one have the power to break it?
In time, does it fade?
Can you tell your heart to stop loving the other?
Will it listen?

The Problem

Apart from Him, I can do nothing.
Apart from him and I feel nothing.
A part of me was found in him
now he's gone, it's missing.
I woke up that morning with sickness in my
stomach.
Butterflies that died because your lies harvested.
They sprouted. They grew.
I'm sure it hurts to tell the truth.
You never did.
So who do I blame for my pain?
Was the truth always there but I just didn't care?
Because a part of you was better than being apart
from you.
So now I date and I take the same place because
I'm scarred.
I'm scared that everyone is like you.
They're all liars sent to destroy me.
Leave me fragile, unbearable.
I'm never having children.
I'm never getting married
cause see I'll never love another
because I'll never give another
the chance to hurt me like you.
It's about time I stop loving someone I was never
good enough for.

Peace

Hear That?

Silence. No chaos.
My spirit is at rest.
No warnings,
telling me to flee, to escape,
because sin is crouched at the gate.
I feel safe with you.
Every moment is easy; it's peace.

Protection

Grotesque gray,
the sky on that Friday.

Excited to be going on my first date-
I didn't ask permission.

What harm could it do?
I know you, you go to my school.

Going on a date with a jock.
I kinda still can't believe you noticed me.

Movie day and burger night,
I'm really enjoying my time.

My curfew is approaching,
so it's about time for my retreat.

You slid in to make a home run,
I curled up on the backseat.

Feeling as if I were shredding
the one thing I thought I owned, stolen.
A porcupine rose set free to cause havoc.

Unfinished

Beavers build dams with ease because there's
nothing coming.

The levee breaks and here comes the flood.
It has been held.

If my best is not enough then I have nothing left to
give.

Spades

We were playing cards.
You had spades, I had hearts.
Silly me because I thought you'd never cut me.
It's the move you can never see coming.

I thought you should always be able to trust your
partner.
I thought there was some type of secret aroma in
the air that says, "Do not cross this line."

I had meticulously, examined the moves being
played.
I stayed away from any that would cross you.
I maneuvered in such a way that we could win with
ease.
It appears, winning wasn't up your sleeve.

We could've set them, I even saw that I could call
renig, but in my glorious moment,
the one I was going to own it,
all with.
Did the unforgivable, with hearts leading,
your spaded Joker floated over my hearted Queen.
She was strong enough to win.
But you weren't paying attention.

Loading

Anticipating,
sitting,
tapping,
gazing,
at this screen.
My software is taking forever.
This process of patience has run thin.
I'm excited when you come close to completion
but then let down again.
Freeze,
pause,
and sometimes,
nothing at all.
But somehow I stay
and I wait
hoping,
praying,
one day,
you will finish what we started.
Download failed.

Celebrity

It's like walking outside to enter my car
then driving to school and sitting in an auditorium
Naked.
Pupils and peripherals all on me because I forgot
something sacred.
This exposition, my whole life is exposed.
Can somebody please just help me get some
clothes?
Nobody helps, cause they all are too busy staring.
They're too busy texting, my private moments are
now up for sharing.
It's gone viral, it won't ever come back.
Did I read this part in my contract?
Now I'm public scrutiny.
If I mess up, the world judges me.
Just this once can somebody cut me some slack?
Can somebody see that I've been fighting?
I've been trying.
Nobody sees... 'til the story reads:
CELEBRITY OVERDOSES.
She's dying.

Vitiligo

When you're born you don't realize you're different.
You don't see white or black.
Society teaches you that.
See me, I'm both.
But no, not mixed.
God forgot that part.
Vanilla swirl, zebra, cow, moose, pig.
Can somebody please tell these kids,
a moose isn't mixed?
Or doesn't have spots.
That's what they are.
Some groups call us lady bugs.
I guess it's just another way to make some pretty of all of it.
I feel pretty; I feel unique.
I feel everyone stares at me when I don't have my skin covered.
She was burned.
It's a birthmark, or maybe it's just weird scars.
The doctors say they can make me like Michael Jackson - make me one color.
I've never had a white face before, will I love her?
They say if I changed, my heart would still remain the same, but would she be me?
Will I get special treatment that I haven't all my life?
Because now I'm white.

Awaken

They said he must be special to make you break in
such a way.
I was bold, confident, and not looking for love.
Single, happy, and not even looking to play.
And then life hit me, as it always does.
I started to want, I wanted to indulge.
If I could ever find perfection in this human world,
it was plastered on your erection inside this broken
girl.
Have you ever just wanted to kiss someone's
tattoos?
Your body art, that moves with you,
so true, you do awaken me.
I'm quaking, I'm shaking, you're so elevating.
Control me, hold me, chaining.
Forever changing.
You're up then you're down.
The hardest to figure out.
We pray, you won't stay, you leave, you're back.
The cycle, you must break.
You can't push me away.
The feen, I'm in need, I'll plead,
I'll bleed, I'll die, if you leave.
You have awakened me.

Nostalgia

Ice bar.
Ice box.
Tell me if these words mean anything to you.
Silver spoon.
Tattoos.
Spoiled rotten.
Springs of holly.
Mexican jolly.
Nostalgia, nostalgia, nostalgia.
Remember me?
The memory.
You feel it; you can smell it.
Wake up, wake up, wake up.
Your coffee in the AM.
8 o' clock, you rise.
3 o' clock, you call.
Come to me, come with me, come.
Nostalgia, nostalgia, nostalgia.
Yes fish, no sushi.
A beating, but no bruising.
Blue dragons, scorpions, eagles.
Crown, royal, regal
Dark house, red lights.
Teeth marks, no bites.
Nostalgia, nostalgia, nostalgia.

Double Standards

It's wrong to say, "Hey, you're too fat."
But okay to say, "Hey, you're too skinny."
I've been eating.
Maybe my metabolism is just too fast.
There goes the girl with the big butt again, mines is nice, just not as noticeable.
It's average.
I have an average booty.
Just not a stop and stare booty.
No guy will get slapped if he's caught looking at my booty.
They say if you wanna gain weight, eat more.
And if you're fat – eat less.
Back away from the table, chunky monkey.
See the problem is it's always easier said than done.
I guess it's not right to joke on a fat person cause they're insecure ,
but have you tried sitting in a room -a size two- with chicks with no stomach but -a size 8-.
Some are even -10's and 12's- but from their waist you couldn't tell.
They don't have one.
And here I go seeming to blow away any second now.
But oh trust me the fat girl in the room is just as sad.
Double standards they're everywhere.
If I can't say you're too fat then just stop saying

I'm too skinny.
Pizza?

Convenient

I'm *convenient*, it's not that I'm really needed.
I'm near and your bad ways, I don't correct. *I'm lenient*.
I don't challenge you. I don't make you strive for any goals.
I'm *easy*, whatever you say goes.
I sit in the house and feel *invisible* sometimes.
You're here, but somehow you don't feel like *mines*.
You don't seem to want me. You leave; I stay.
We've put in too much *time* for me to find someone else.
I know there's other women, but I'm okay with getting what's left.
When they're all occupied, I always get my time.
I can tell you love *her* more than me, the way you *smile* when someone mentions her name.
But she's *inconvenient* and she doesn't give you your way. Her very essence makes you want to *change* but you're not ready yet, so I'm *chosen*.
I'm near. I'm here. I'm easy. I'm simple.
I'm convenient.
You cheat and everyone knows it.
You're not here because you *love* me.
You're here because of my conveniency.
There may come a day when you wake and say,
you wasted a lot of years *tolerating* me.
But see, your inconvenient girl has now moved on.
She was way *too smart* to wait for you to grow up.

You *lost* your chance with her because you
couldn't love her when she needed you worst.
So now you're *stuck* with me, this is how I *win* the
guy.
It's easy; it's simple.
 I just had to stay in the fight.
See now, *you **need me***, you've changed.
They got tired of your games.
We may never really be together and *love* it.
But we'll grow old pretending in this *covenant*.

Innate

I had you healthy and gorgeous and then you
destroyed it.
Why'd you go back to what had you broken?
I built you up and made you strong.
I made you feel invincible.
But it's safe to say all I did was restore you until
you got enough strength to leave me.
You suffered severely with her because she isn't
meant for you.
Stop trying to control what your body feels, how
your body reacts to me, you'll come back naturally.
Natural, you were created for me.
It's sad that you're the last to see.
So you sneak behind my back, planning my
demise.
The one that healed you, we were despised.
Everyone wanted to know how to get like us but
you just cut up.
You do the unthinkable, my back turned, you pull
this issue.
Tresses on the ground, I can't stand the same, what
did you do to me?
You're just going to leave me here? I'm dying.
You're just going to invite her back? She's lying.
She's crack to your body. Or have you forgot?
And to make matters worse you have the nerve to
brag in my face.
The compliments from the world have you out of
place.

They've went to your head and you still don't see.
They only congratulate you because you're where
they can be.
Anyone can have her, she's not special.
Even people who struggle in this area can
accomplish that look there.
When you had me it was different, not everyone
could pull it off so beautifully.
You knew me, I knew you.
We were so fruitful we just grew and grew until the
night you wanted something new.
You wanted different, you said I had gotten plain.
 I didn't see this coming I still thought you were
partially sane.
The tyranny, the irony.
She destroys you, you destroy me, undeniably.
She's manufactured, she's fake.
I don't need to be seen to place in this race.
Cause even when they think I've lost I'm building.
 I'm getting stronger underneath it all.
As time goes on, I let you move on thinking you've
made the right decision.
I can't make you stay with me, although I made
you healthy.
But see you can never stop what you're going to do
naturally.

Pretty at the Bus Stop

This is the moment you realize you don't have any friends.

On your way to the top everyone just can't grow with you.

Everyone looks at you with your nice clothes and your hair done saying,

"Either she's lost or her priorities are basic."

It's neither.

You weren't given a silver spoon so you grind.

You hear the shade of those acting as if this is your destination.

Honey, you're going places and this bus is the beginning.

See, unlike those people who were given everything …

You'll always remember when you had nothing.

Humbled.

Conditionally

Do you love me?
Like really love me?
I find myself asking these questions.
It appears you're always by my side, so helpful.
But is it possible to love selfishly?
See as time goes, your love seems to be
conditioned.
You love me enough to get me to please you but in
an instance you've changed.
We don't go out anymore, you never invite me to
your events, there's someone new, but you still say
you love me.

You love us in different ways and you say I'll
always have a place.
We've been in this for over a decade but I just
figured out the cycle.
I use to laugh and joke about how you did other
people...
straddling them along until they served their
purpose in your life.
You'd then cut them off, cold.
The emotions had gotten old, you no longer could
use them.
I saw you repeat this cycle over and over.
I even knew when the chopping block was coming.
I never knew I was on this block, I thought you
loved me differently.
This caricature I had of you wouldn't hurt me, this

is just funny.
But your character is where I just shouldn't have bet money.
This is you.
You're this way to everyone, how could I be so dumb.....to think I was different.

Diamond

I stopped caring yesterday.
I deleted your thread.
I stopped caring yesterday.
I blocked your number like you said.
I stopped caring yesterday.
I quit reminiscing on the good moments.
I stopped caring yesterday.
I won't be on Instagram reading all your
comments.
I stopped caring yesterday.
When I took that final blow.
I stopped caring yesterday.
No more making excuses for you.
I stopped caring yesterday.
Yes, I know you've been hurt.
I stopped caring yesterday.
I got mistreated for those scars and that's worst.
I stopped caring yesterday.
Maybe your boys can fulfill all your needs.
I stopped caring yesterday.
They always got more time than me.
I stopped caring yesterday.
You're stupid for throwing away a diamond.
I stopped caring yesterday.
You lost my value but I'll still have worth to the
person who finds me.
I stopped caring yesterday.
I really did fight for this thing.
I stopped caring yesterday.

I'm so wounded I don't even want to throw another
swing.
I stopped caring yesterday.
Seems like I finally got the hint.
I stopped caring yesterday.
Only I still thought we were meant.
I stopped caring yesterday.
I'll cry about it tonight.
I stopped caring yesterday.
And in the morning everything will be alright.
I stopped caring yesterday.

Reciprocity

I was hoping for love.
But all you were giving me was sex and attention.
On lonely nights it felt about equal.
I guess it wasn't right for me to ask you to wear a
shoe you never agreed to.
I didn't realize 'til now but that's what I really
wanted -love- but since I couldn't see it.
You were what I filled the void with.
Well I tried it, you just wouldn't fit.
My cup was always on empty.
There was no peace, only pressure of me trying to
convince myself that this was actually working.
I was searching for love but I settled for you.
You couldn't give what you didn't have.
I don't blame you for being who you were.
 I blame me for acting like I couldn't see it.
You let me live. You were always right.
You let me learn. You always warned.
I gave it, myself to many.
I always felt empty.
Reciprocity?
Can someone show it?
They say men use love to get sex and women use
sex to get love.
With hidden motives already in play,
it seems lies is all we reciprocate.

Vision

I don't want to go to hell.
I mean...if hell is real.
They say it is.
Is god even real?
They say he is.
I get a peace from some mystery being here.
I think.
If god is real, why is this world so cruel?
Why do people hate me...if god is love?
There goes that queer, so gay he can't see straight,
but my vision is perfect.
Unlike this world, these people, they're not perfect.
Their sins are hidden.
They're struggling, silently.
I'm the brave one.
I put it out there.
I let you see the real me.
Born this way. I won't change.
Oh look there goes the Pharisees judging me every
time I enter a room.
This room is silent but their thoughts scream
damnation, abomination.
Yes, this is my thorn in my side, I've tried.
I've cried. I've prayed.
But it won't go away.
So I'm ridiculed, I'm the fool cause I'm choosing
hell.
I'm the pregnant girl in the room with no ring
because see we both have obviously sinned.

Released

I loved you more than my life.
I might've betrayed myself or my God for you.
I said I didn't want a piece of you but then I got a
piece of you and I was hooked again.
Bait for the fish, I'm caught in your web.
This feels like home, but I think I've been robbed.
We're here but something is missing.
You left part of your love with her.
I have been in this more times than I care to admit.
I am sick of this.
When we meet, I still don't feel complete.
I feel used.
My heart can't take this a day longer.
I love you, I want you, but not in these
circumstances.
Since it's hard for you to pick,
I'll choose for you.
You are released from me
and finally in my life,
I feel released from you.
I'm free.

www.ingramcontent.com/pod-product-compliance
Lightning Source LLC
Chambersburg PA
CBHW020448030426
42337CB00014B/1455